THE
LITTLE SPICE
BOOK

Rosamond Richardson

PIATKUS

© 1988 Judy Piatkus (Publishers) Limited

First published in 1988 by
Judy Piatkus (Publishers) Limited,
5 Windmill Street, London W1P 1HF

British Library Cataloguing in Publication Data
Richardson, Rosamond, *1945–*
The little spice book.
1. Spices
I. Title
641.3′383

ISBN 0-86188-725-5

Drawings by Rosamond Richardson
Designed by Susan Ryall
Cover photograph by Theo Bergström

Phototypeset in 10 on 11pt Linotron Plantin by
Phoenix Photosetting, Chatham
Printed and bound in Great Britain by
The Bath Press, Avon

CONTENTS

INTRODUCING SPICES

By definition, spices are strongly flavoured aromatic substances of vegetable origin obtained from tropical plants. A spice can be fruit, flower, flower-bud, stigma, seed, root or bark of the plant. All except three of the most important spices come from the Orient; the exceptions – allspice, capsicum and vanilla – come from the tropics of Central America.

Spices have a romantic and exotic history: myths and legends were created around them – some by traders who wished to obscure the whereabouts of the spice from rivals, others out of wonder at the uniqueness of spices – and they became associated with imaginary beasts like the phoenix, dragon and fabulous serpents.

Throughout their history spices have been deemed more precious than herbs, even in their countries of origin. Although, surprisingly, they do not feature in literature to anything like the same extent as herbs, yet they were thought of as just as mystical – and used accordingly in worship, rituals and healing.

SPICES IN HISTORY

The earliest written allusions to spices are in the Old Testament – the journey of the Queen of Sheba to King Solomon in Jerusalem in 950 BC was ostensibly to develop trade relations over the spice routes, from which a considerable part of the king's immense income came.

Throughout the first and second millennia BC, Arabia prospered as the carrier of this precious cargo from East to West. By means of donkey caravan she plied her trade from Cathay bearing cinnamon, cassia, cardamom, frankincense, ginger and turmeric. The Arabians were shrewd traders and artfully withheld the source of their goods, giving rise to numerous legends; they claimed cinnamon, for example, was only to be found in deep valleys infested with poisonous snakes, and grew only in Africa. Their ploy was successful and they monopolized the trade for many centuries.

In India, excavations in the Indus valley reveal that herbs and spices were being used more than 1,000 years before Christ. Ayurvedic medicine, an ancient form of Hindu practice, includes many spices in its system, and other very early herbal systems in India included cardamom, ginger, black pepper, cumin and mustard seed among cures for such diverse complaints as obesity, urinary infection, piles and jaundice.

Alexander the Great (356–323 BC), in his attempt to extend classical Greek influence, reached the Indus valley and stumbled upon a hitherto undreamt-of possibility, a direct route for trade in spices with the East. From then on spices became known all over the classical world. (Hippocrates, the 'Father of Modern Medicine', includes saffron, cinnamon, coriander, pepper and ginger in his 400 simples or 'useful plants'.)

The Romans, as the Greeks had done, realized that the Arabians were demanding extortionate prices, and by the time of Pliny the Elder (AD 23–70) they were ridiculing their tales of 'fabulous beasts'. They began to trade with India, breaking the Arab monopoly and bringing prices down considerably.

It would appear that it was the Romans who first experimented with spices in cooking in the West – they ate spicy pickled foods, and the great gourmet and writer Apicius included pepper, turmeric and ginger in his recipes. Spiced wine was popular and the Romans also scented their baths with aromatic oils, lit lamps with essential oils, and used spices in their 'strewings'.

With the fall of Rome in the 5th century AD came the rise of Islam. Mohammed had been a cameldriver in control of the trade caravan of a rich widow whom he married in 594 AD. After his marriage, and before his divine revelation, he dealt in spices and frankincense in Mecca. The Islamic world went on to dominate the spice trade for a time.

The Crusades against the Infidel which started in the 11th century meant the introduction of spices into Western Europe by returning Crusaders. By the 13th century spices were becoming a feature – albeit a luxury – of many a well-to-do household. But it is quite probable that the dreadful plagues which decimated medieval Europe were carried by rats brought to the West on the spice ships – a high price to pay. Yet it was to the antiseptic qualities of these very spices that the victims turned for help – they wore nosebags filled with spices to prevent infection, and bathed with sponges soaked in extracts of cloves and cinnamon.

The takeover by Venice of the spice trade, particularly pepper, in the 13th century, led directly to the great voyages of discovery which opened up the world. Columbus, Vasco da Gama and Magellan were all inspired by the lure of the riches which spices brought – to discover routes to the East. Magellan himself was killed in a skirmish with natives of the Spice Islands. The 16th and 17th centuries saw a struggle for power between the Portuguese, Dutch and British, all of whom wanted in turn to monopolize the trade. The story of spices is written in blood.

Spices have remained an enormous economic force in the development of the world, and are today an important money-making concern on the commodities market.

SPICES IN FOLK MEDICINE

The medicinal values of spices are generally less important in the history of healing than those of herbs, yet some have featured in pharmacopoeias and one of them, the poppy, has supplied mankind with one of its most powerful narcotics, morphine.

The property that spices have in common with each other is that they act on the digestive system: many of them relieve wind and flatulence, and a few have laxative effects. They are all termed aromatic stimulants, and are used as tonics to tone up the system, and several of them are used in chest complaints.

Some of the early herbalists have exaggerated their efficacy, calling them panaceas for all ills (including the 'bitings of madde dogges' and the venomous sting of the scorpion). Then there was the doctrine of signatures: because of its colour, turmeric was thought to be good for jaundice; and because of its shape, the clove was used as an aphrodisiac – all uncertain, not to say whimsical, claims.

Several spices have been used in veterinary medicine in the past, but generally speaking this, as with their uses in human medicine, is minimal and relatively insignificant in medical history.

Spices In Cooking And Other Uses

Spices are of central importance in the great Oriental cuisines of the world. Chinese cooking could not exist without ginger, that of the Middle East without cumin, and the characteristic heat of Indian dishes depends heavily on chillies, cloves and turmeric. Some of the most famous dishes of Western gastronomy are centred around a spice: *bouillabaisse* and *paella* both rely on saffron, Hungarian *goulash* on paprika, English mincemeat on ground cloves and cinnamon, and *steak au poivre* on black peppercorns. Mulled spiced wines have been enjoyed for centuries, and aromatic seeds like cumin, poppy and sesame have been used both on and in breads, cakes and pastries. Mixed spice is an important flavouring in mass-produced ketchups and sauces, sausages and salamis, and many spices are important ingredients of pickles and preserves.

Spices play a vital part in flavouring some of the world's greatest liqueurs – *absinthe, anisette*, Benedictine, Curaçao, Kümmel, Pernod and *ouzo* are all produced with the use of spices. They have also been used to flavour tobaccos, and some play their part in confectionery too.

The essential oils of spices are widely used in perfumery and cosmetics – in hair oils, soaps and toilet preparations, as well as toothpastes and breath-fresheners. Many are powerfully antiseptic and make good insecticides. Oils from certain spices were mixed into candle wax or just lit on their own as illuminants. The oils have found their way into margarines, domestic cleaners, pharmaceuticals and dyes.

Spices have been burnt as incense ever since they were first discovered, giving off their beautiful scents – which in less hygienic days was not so much a bonus as a necessity. They were used among strewing herbs, in elegant *pot-pourris* and aromatic sachets.

ALLSPICE

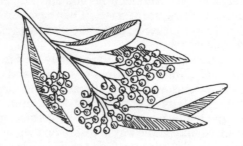

Allspice is the highly aromatic berry of the pimento tree, a tropical evergreen of the myrtle family, and is one of only three major spices to be grown commercially in the Western hemisphere. Jamaica is one of the principal sources of world supplies.

The annual average yield of a mature tree is in the region of 150 lb (67.5 kg). The nearly-ripe berries are harvested in June, and then are either sun-dried or kiln-dried.

The French call allspice *quatre épices* because of the flavour, which seems to combine those of cinnamon, cloves, ginger and nutmeg. 'Jamaica pepper' is one of its local names, because the spice so closely resembles peppercorns in appearance. Indeed the first European to discover allspice, an explorer called Francisco Hernandez, named it *Piper tabasci* for the same reason.

The first record of its import into Europe is in

1601, and by 1739 regular shipments were being made into England. It was widely used as a preservative, and this custom still lingers in Scandinavia where the berries are used to preserve fish in barrels *en route* to the coastal markets of the Baltic.

From the earliest times allspice was considered a cure-all, and found its way into numerous pharmacopoeias. It is an aromatic stimulant and carminative, good for flatulence, indigestion and hysterical paroxysms. It also played a part in the treatment of rheumatism and neuralgia. The powdered berries were used to disguise the taste of disagreeable medicines!

The essential oil of allspice is used in aromatics, in the manufacture of soaps and perfumes. Allspice is also used to flavour the liqueurs Benedictine and Chartreuse. Pimento wood was once used for the manufacture of umbrella handles and walking sticks.

Allspice is one of the principal pickling spices. The berry, ground, is an important ingredient of mixed spice, and is used to flavour ketchups and soups, salamis, sausages and pork pies. It is versatile, as delicious with sweet foods as savoury, often used in mincemeat and Christmas puddings, for example, and is delicious with both fruit and vegetable dishes.

ALLSPICE HERRINGS

So characteristic of Scandinavian food, these allspice-flavoured herrings make a delicious picnic dish, or a simple lunch served with fresh wholemeal bread and a green salad. The spicing transforms the fish and gives them a pungent, aromatic quality.

4 large herrings, filleted
1 large onion, peeled and finely chopped
10 allspice berries
6 peppercorns
2 bay leaves
2 sprigs thyme
1 pint (600 ml) white wine vinegar
1 tablespoon salt

Cut the herring fillets into strips. Put them into jars with the chopped onion, allspice berries, peppercorns, bay leaves and thyme. Pour the vinegar over the top, add the salt and close the jars securely. Give them a good shake, then store in a cool place for up to 4 weeks – or even longer in the fridge.

Makes 2 × 2 lb (900 g) jars

ANISE

Anise was used in biblical days as a tithe, and was cultivated by the ancient Egyptians, Greeks and Romans. By the Middle Ages its cultivation spread to central Europe through Spain, and it was grown in England from the 12th century onwards. It is an annual umbellifer, growing up to 2 feet (60 cm) high, with flat yellow umbels of flowers. It gives its characteristic flavour to all the anise drinks of the Mediterranean – *anisette*, Pernod, *ouzo* and *arrak*. The seed is used in confectionery, in cakes, biscuits and vegetable curries, and flavours *anisbrod*, a German bread. Medicinally it is used to relieve flatulence, as an ingredient in cough mixtures, and for bronchitis and asthma. They say that hanging anise next to your pillow will keep away bad dreams!

CAPSICUM

The capsicum or pepper belongs to a large plant family native to tropical America which includes potatoes, tomatoes, aubergines and the tobacco plant. Capsicums come in all shapes and sizes, from bulbous and rounded to long and pointed. Their flavours vary from the hottest to the mildest, and colours range through red, orange, yellow, purple, cream and green. The shrubs on which they grow are both deciduous and evergreen, and little miniature ones can be grown from seed as pot plants.

There are about fifty different varieties of peppers: the two major varieties are fresh bell or sweet peppers, which are eaten as vegetables, either raw or cooked, and chillies, which lend their heat to hot Mexican dishes and Indian curries. Other varieties, dried, yield the hot spices associated with national specialities all over the world – cayenne, Tabasco, chilli powder or seasoning, and paprika.

Archaeological evidence shows that peppers were cultivated 9,000 years ago in Peru and Mexico, but they did not become known in the West until after the discovery of the Americas by Columbus. He reported that 'There is much *axi*, which is their pepper, and it is stronger than pepper, and the people won't eat without it, for they find it so very wholesome.' A classic recipe called *mole*, a hot pepper sauce of which the natives were evidently proud, was offered to the Spanish explorer Cortez in

the 16th century. By 1618 capsicums could be bought at Billingsgate, where they were known as Guinea or Ginnie peppers, and in powdered form they appear in 18th- and 19th-century recipe books.

The ancient Indian medical treatise, the *Ayurveda*, recommends chillies as an aid to digestion and a cure for paralysis. They were also used to cure cramp and diarrhoea, and West Indians use chillies as a gargle for a sore throat. Peppers stimulate gastric secretion, promote sweating, and activate a sluggish digestion. Bell peppers have a very high vitamin C content as well as containing vitamins A and E, so are nutritionally valuable.

Capsicums were said in folklore to offer protection against werewolves and vampires. The Aztecs used chillies to punish wayward children by holding them over the spice as it was burning! And there is a South American Indian punishment for flirtation: if a girl so much as looked at a man she had chilli rubbed into her eyes. If she slept with him, the punishment was accordingly worse . . .

Fresh bell peppers have a pungent taste which lingers long on the palate, and are widely used in salads and added to casseroles. They are also delicious stuffed and baked. Fresh chilli peppers are also eaten raw (with caution!) and cooked.

Capsicum oil is a common ingredient of hair lotions as it stimulates the growth of the hair. It is also used in soaps and candles, and gives a sharp flavour to ginger ale and ginger beer.

SPICY STUFFED PEPPERS

These stuffed peppers have a Middle-Eastern quality to them, spiced with cumin, coriander and chilli powder, with added pine nuts. A delicious supper dish, served with a crisp green salad.

1 large onion, peeled and finely chopped
3 tablespoons vegetable oil
6 oz (175 g) rice, washed
1/2 pint (300 ml) stock
6 oz (175 g) mushrooms, finely chopped
2 oz (50 g) pine nuts, browned under the grill
1/2 teaspoon each chilli powder and turmeric
1 teaspoon each ground cumin and coriander
salt
4 medium bell peppers, halved lengthwise and seeded

Cook the onion in the oil for 5–6 minutes until it begins to soften, then stir in the rice. Cook until coated with the oil, about 3 minutes, and add half the stock gradually, stirring for 3–4 minutes more. Stir in the mushrooms, and add the pine nuts, the spices and salt to taste.

Heap this spiced rice mixture into the pepper halves and arrange in a lightly greased baking dish. Pour over the rest of the stock. Cover with foil and bake at 325°F/160°C/Gas 3 for 45–50 minutes until tender, basting every 10 minutes or so. Cool a little and serve warm.

Serves 4

CARAWAY

An umbellifer with small white umbels of flowers, caraway bears little crescent-shaped seeds about ¼ inch (5 mm) long, which are used to flavour breads and cheeses, cabbage dishes and soups. They can be used whole or ground, and are an important ingredient of the liqueur, Kümmel. Used medicinally to calm the digestive system, they cure flatulence and indigestion, and feature in many children's medicines. The spice has been used for at least 5,000 years; in ancient Egypt, then by the Romans – Julius Caesar's soldiers ate a bread made of caraway roots mixed with milk – and was well known to Shakespeare. Up until the end of the last century caraway seed cake was traditional fare at celebratory feasts given by farmers for their labourers at the end of wheat sowing. In America caraway seeds were given to children to chew during long Sunday sermons – and were called 'meetin' seeds'.

CARDAMOM

Cardamom is native to the evergreen monsoon forests of Southern India, and it also grows wild in Burma. It is cultivated commercially in India, Sri Lanka and Guatemala, whence comes some of the finest quality cardamom. It is an herbaceous perennial plant of the ginger family which produces slightly pungent, highly aromatic pods containing seeds with a camphor-like flavour. These pods are picked just before maturity and washed with water from special wells. They are then sun-dried, and bleached for marketing. Green or white cardamoms are the most common; brown or black cardamoms are much larger and more pungent.

There are several references to cardamom as an aphrodisiac in the *Arabian Nights*, and in many parts of the East it was considered sacred and used in sacrifices. It was said to have been cultivated, with turmeric, in the gardens of Babylon in the 8th century BC, and the Egyptians chewed cardamom seeds to keep their teeth white.

Cardamom was an important item of trade for the Greeks in the 4th century BC, carefully graded by quality. It was the most popular of the aromatic spices in ancient Rome, highly praised by the gastronome Apicius, and by the 1st century AD large quantities were being imported from India. It was later to become popular in Western Europe: in the 17th century, the Portuguese who had colonized the Malabar Coast collected cardamom and exported it from India and Ceylon.

Medicinally, cardamom is an aromatic stimulant which acts on the digestive system and is good for colic, indigestion and flatulence. It is purgative, and has also been used in the treatment of piles, jaundice and disorders of the head. The earliest records of Ayurvedic medicine in India, dating back to the 4th century BC, mention cardamom as being used for urinary complaints, and for removing fat.

Cardamom is very popular in Arab countries today, especially in Saudi Arabia where they make a special 'cardamom coffee' (sometimes also flavoured with saffron or ground cloves) which they call *gahira*. It is an important symbol of hospitality and is poured with ceremonial ritual, the host moving among his guests to serve them according to rank or status.

Cardamom is an important ingredient of many Near and Far Eastern dishes, particularly the curries and *pullaos* of Northern India, and it is also widely used to flavour traditional sweetmeats. It is a luxury ingredient of the India *pa'an*, wrapped in betel leaves and slowly chewed after meals as a digestive. In Egypt the seeds are ground and put into coffee, and they are as delicious in mulled wine. Try cardamom in an apple pie, or in a meat loaf, for it is as good in savoury as in sweet dishes. It gives chicken a delicate and original flavour, and is lovely in fruit salads or a grape jelly. It is also good in pickles, in hot punches and wine. It features in some Middle-European meat dishes and lends its characteristic flavour to Scandinavian pastries.

Green cardamoms are roughly oval in shape and about ½ inch (1 cm) long. They are lightly ridged, and when dried they split open easily to reveal half a dozen or so black, highly pungent seeds. The pods can be used whole, slightly bruised, to give flavour to marinating or cooking foods, and are then removed before eating. Alternatively, the seeds are ground and the spice is sold in powdered form. Ground black cardamoms are used in garam masala.

The essential oil of cardamom is used in perfumery in France and the United States, and also in some scented domestic articles.

PEAR TART WITH CARDAMOM

1/2 pint (300 ml) red wine
2 tablespoons lemon juice
4 green cardamom seeds
5 oz (150 g) granulated sugar
1 1/2 lb (750 g) ripe pears, peeled, cored and quartered
5 tablespoons redcurrant jelly
1 × 10 inch (25 cm) sweet pastry case, baked blind
1 large carton Greek yogurt
shredded almonds, toasted, to garnish

Put the red wine, lemon juice, cardamom seeds and sugar into a heavy pan and bring to the boil, stirring until the sugar dissolves. Then bring to a rapid boil and cook for 5 minutes until a syrup is formed. Poach the pear quarters in the syrup for about 8 minutes and then leave to cool in the syrup for 5 minutes. Life them out carefully with a slotted spoon and drain thoroughly.

Boil the remaining syrup to thread stage (446°F/230°C) and strain off 5 tablespoons. Mix this with the redcurrant jelly and heat together until the jelly dissolves and the glaze coats the back of a spoon.

Paint the inside of the pastry shell with the glaze and leave to cool for an hour. Cover with the Greek yogurt. Slice the pears lengthwise and arrange over the top. Decorate with the browned shredded almonds and serve chilled.

Serves 6–8

CINNAMON

Cinnamon (or its close relative, cassia) was known to the Chinese as long ago as 2,500 BC, and in its early history was more precious than gold. It was a valuable commodity in ancient Arabia where priests alone had the right to collect it: the first bundle was offered to the sun, and was then used to kindle the sacred fire on the altar where the high priest was to offer sacrifice. The ancient Egyptians used cinnamon for embalming and in witchcraft, and in 1485 BC Queen Hatshepsut is reported as despatching rigged ships to the land of Punt (Somalia) to bring back frankincense, cinnamon, baboons, dogs and myrrh.

First documented as a product of Ceylon in 1275, cinnamon was to play a vital role in bringing the East into contact with Europe. Up until that time all spices were supposed to have come from the Garden of Eden by way of the Euphrates, 'a river which floweth from paradise'. When the Portuguese landed in Ceylon in 1500 they found cinnamon growing in the wild, and by 1536 they were occupying the country, mainly to obtain supplies of the spice. The King of Ceylon was forced to pay to the Portuguese an annual tribute of 25,000 pounds of cinnamon bark! In 1796 Ceylon passed into British hands and cinnamon became a monopoly of the British East India Company, and so remained until 1833.

Today the spice is cultivated in Java, Burma, South America and the West Indies, a bushy, evergreen tree of the laurel family. One acre will yield between 100 and 150 lb (45–67.5 kg) stick cinnamon. The spice consists of the inner bark: the shoots are peeled, then rubbed to loosen the bark which is split and peeled. The peels are then telescoped into one another to form a quill about 42 inches (1 metre) long, before being dried and bleached ready for marketing.

One of the many legends concerning cinnamon says that it was gathered from the nest of the phoenix, miraculous bird of ancient fable, that collected cinnamon, spikenard and myrrh to fuel the magic fire in which it would cremate itself and from which it would be reborn.

Cinnamon is an antiseptic spice and relieves flatulence and nausea. It was a treatment for diarrhoea and internal bleeding, and has been given as a sedative in labour. The ancient Greeks prescribed cinnamon in hot rum as a cure for a cold, an unbeatable remedy even today.

Cinnamon is used in baking cakes and biscuits, and is delicious in fruit puddings and pastries. Rice pudding is transformed with the addition of cinnamon, and cinnamon ice cream is Epicurean. The spice is also used to flavour liqueurs and confectionery, soaps and toothpastes. The oil it contains is eugenol, an effective breath-freshener, so you can chew a stick of cinnamon for instant sweet breath!

CINNAMON FOR LUSTROUS BROWN HAIR

You can make a hair-rinse with cinnamon which is particularly good for highlighting brown hair. It also smells wonderful! Infuse 1 oz (25 g) stick cinnamon in 1 pint (600 ml) hot water (just below simmering point) for 10 minutes, and then leave to cool, covered. Strain off and bottle.

To use, pour 2–3 tablespoons on to the scalp after shampooing, rubbing it in thoroughly with the fingertips. Leave to work for about 10 minutes before rinsing.

CINNAMON COOKIES

Crisp and light, these delectable spicy cookies are a delicious tea-time snack, especially on the day that they are made (I find they never last longer than anyway – a clean sweep is the usual fate of these biscuits). They are also lovely served with ice cream.

3 oz (75 g) caster sugar
2 oz (50 g) margarine or butter
4 oz (100 g) flour
2 teaspoons powdered cinnamon

Cream the sugar with the margarine or butter. Sift the flour with the cinnamon and beat into the creamed mixture. Roll into 12 small balls and place on a greased baking tray. Press them down in the middle with a fork, and bake in a preheated oven at 350°F/180°C/Gas 4 for 8–10 minutes until golden. Cool on a rack.

Makes 12

HOT CHOCOLATE WITH CINNAMON

For a nightcap this takes some beating. Just stirring a hot chocolate milk drink with a stick of cinnamon infuses it with a delicate suggestion of the spice which is far from overpowering. It is wonderful – and the scoop of ice cream on the top ensures against night starvation!

¾ pint (450 ml) milk
2 tablespoons chocolate powder
2 scoops soft ice cream
2 × 6 inch (15 cm) sticks cinnamon

Heat the milk to boiling point and pour into two mugs. Sprinkle the hot chocolate powder over the top and stir with the cinnamon sticks until it dissolves. Leave the cinnamon sticks in the hot chocolate for 3–4 minutes until it becomes cool enough to drink, then float a scoop of soft ice cream on the top of each. Serve with the cinnamon stick still in the mug, to stir in the melting ice cream.

Serves 2

24

CLOVES

In 1519 Magellan set sail westwards, the first man to sail around Cape Horn, eventually to reach the Moluccas or Spice Islands. In 1522 his ship returned to Europe laden with cloves, and his countrymen, the Portuguese, dominated trade with the Spice Islands until they were expelled by the Dutch in 1605. The new colonists restricted the cultivation of cloves to one island in an attempt to keep them scarce and the price high, but seeds were smuggled out to Mauritius in the 18th century and by 1800 were being grown in Zanzibar as well. In 1795 the British planted clove trees in Penang, which to this day have continued to bear cloves of the highest quality.

The trees of which cloves are the flower-buds are pretty, pyramidal evergreens which reach to about 30 feet (9 metres) in height, and live to a good old age. They start flowering in their fifth year, and women beat the unopened buds off the stalks during the season which lasts from September to February. The buds are then sun-dried, each tree yielding perhaps up to 75 lb (33.5 kg) of cloves.

The clove is one of the most powerful and pungent of aromatics, used since ancient times for a variety of ailments. In Ayurvedic medicine cloves were prescribed for a huge number of illnesses: for fevers, dyspepsia, disorders of the brain, for toning up the heart, and to relieve kidney, stomach, spleen and intestinal disorders. Oil of cloves has been administered in cases of paralysis, and also for neuralgic pain and rheumatism.

In folk medicine cloves are a classic cure for toothache – old wives recommended soaking them in hot honey and chewing them slowly whilst rolling them around the aching tooth. Some said they were aphrodisiac, others made 'a certain liquor by distillation, or a most fragrant smell, which comforteth the heart, and is of all cordials the most effectual' (Gerard).

Cloves are usually used whole, and in small amounts, but the small head can be crumbled, or the whole bud powdered. They play a part in curries, in pickles (partly as a preservative), and in hot mulls and punches. They can be used for savoury and sweet dishes alike, are widely used in baking, and are a vital ingredient of Christmas mincemeat. A classic use of cloves is in decorating a sugar-coated ham.

Oil of cloves is used in germicides, mouthwashes and toothpastes and is a powerful antiseptic. Aromatic pomanders – an orange stuck with cloves – have been popular for perfuming and moth-proofing chests and wardrobes from medieval days up to the present time.

The natives of the Spice Islands revered clove trees and planted one for the birth of each of their children. If the tree flourished, so would the child. The little ones were also protected both from evil influences and from infantile illnesses by wearing a necklace of cloves. According to the natives, the trees should be planted only when there is no moon, and they must be shaken during an eclipse. They wear the flowers as a mark of distinction, grading their nobles by giving them between one and four, to wear like medals.

A CLOVE SLEEP PILLOW

To induce sleep and fragrant dreams: To well-dried rose petals and sweet briar leaves add dried mint and pounded cloves. Mix well and stuff a small pillow with the mixture.

SPICY CLOVE AND WALNUT BREAD

Eat this soft, aromatic bread warm from the oven. It is easy to make and needs only one rising time, filling the kitchen with mouthwatering smells!

2 eggs
4 oz (100 g) brown sugar
1 lb (500 g) strong flour
1/2 teaspoon salt
2 teaspoons ground cloves
4 teaspoons baking powder
1 pint (600 ml) milk
6 oz (175 g) walnuts, chopped

Beat the eggs well and stir in the sugar. Beat again until thick.

Sift the flour with the salt, cloves and baking powder, and add alternately with the milk to the egg mixture. Stir in the chopped nuts and pour into two well-greased loaf tins.

Leave to stand for 30 minutes, then cook at 350°F/180°C/Gas 4 for 45 minutes. Cool on a rack.

Makes 2 × 1 lb (500 g) loaves

POMANDER

A pomander makes a lovely Christmas gift. Cardinal Wolsey had one tied to his belt on visiting days to keep off the hideous stench of the streets and the less than lovely odours of his parishioners!

1 oz (25 g) whole cloves
1 orange
4 tablespoons orris root powder

Push the cloves into the orange skin so close together that they touch. (If your fingers get sore doing this, poke holes in the fruit with a fine knitting needle.) Leave a band around the vertical circumference of the orange so that you can tie a ribbon around it when it is ready.

When the orange is finished, roll it in the orris root powder until completely coated. Put it into a brown paper bag and place it in a dark cupboard to dry out for 2–3 weeks. Then tie the ribbon around it and hang in a clothes cupboard or anywhere around the house for it to impart its fragrance.

CUMIN

Cumin is an annual plant which originally came from the East, but which has been grown around the Mediterranean for some 2,000 years. It is a typical umbellifer with fine leaves and white or rose-coloured umbels of flowers, rather similar to caraway, with which it is often confused. Its seeds are thin, yellowish brown, elongated ovals about ¼ inch (5 mm) long, lined with ridges, and with a strong, heavy aroma. The plant itself, slender and pretty, grows about 1 foot (30 cm) tall, from as far south as the Nile to as far north as Norway.

Cumin is mentioned as a crop in the Old Testament in the Book of Isaiah, and also in the New Testament as a tithe. Pliny wrote that the ancients took the ground seed medicinally, with bread, water or wine, and that it was not only the best of condiments, but also an excellent appetizer. The Romans apparently used it like we use pepper today, and also made it into a paste for bread.

Records tell us that during the 13th and 14th centuries the average price of cumin on Britain was 2 pennies per pound. By 1419 it was a taxable import in London for Crown income, indicating how it had become an established spice in English life.

It was a spice much used in folk medicine, but nowadays its use is confined mainly to veterinary practice. Cumin mixed with flour and water is good feed for poultry, and they say that if you give tame pigeons cumin it makes them fond of their home and less likely to stray.

Basically stimulant, antispasmodic and carminative in its action, the ancient Hindus used cumin for jaundice and piles, and old European herbalists claimed that it was better for flatulence than either fennel or caraway, and they prescribed it for indigestion and headaches too.

Both whole and powdered cumin seeds are especially popular in Oriental and Latin American cookery, and are ingredients of mixed spice, chutneys, chilli and curry powders. Dutch and Swiss cheeses often have cumin seeds in them as flavouring, and in France and Germany they are popular in cakes and breads. Cumin flavours soups and stews, marinated chicken, *chilli con carne* and meat loaves. It is also delicious in *choucroûte*. Cumin oil is used in perfumery and for flavouring the liqueur Kümmel.

CUMIN LENTILS

This very simple dish, so cheap to make and easy to assemble, is delicious with plain roast chicken or with grilled fish. Spiced with turmeric as well as cumin, it is slightly hot and full of flavour – reminiscent of the Southern Indian cooking which inspired it.

8 oz (250 g) green lentils, soaked for 6 hours in cold water
1 onion, peeled and sliced
1 bay leaf
1 whole fresh chilli pepper
1 inch (2.5 cm) piece fresh root ginger, bruised
1 tablespoon each turmeric and ground cumin
salt

Drain the soaked lentils and boil them in a pan of water to cover, with the onion, bay leaf, chilli and ginger. After about 20 minutes when they are soft, drain off all but a little of the water and add the turmeric and cumin, and salt to taste. Leave to stand, covered with a lid, for about 20 minutes in order to allow all the flavours to blend. Remove the chilli, onion, bay leaf and ginger before serving.

Serves 4

FENUGREEK

Fenugreek is one of the oldest plants in cultivation, used by the ancient Egyptians as incense. The Benedictines grew it during the Dark Ages in Europe, and it was widely grown up until the 19th century. A native of Asia, it is an upright annual with light green leaves and a pod about 6 inches (15 cm) long which contains yellow-brown seeds. These give their flavour to confectionery, and are mixed with bread flour in poor countries to add a pleasantly bitter taste. Its most familiar use is in curry powder, and it is also added to pickles. Used medicinally, fenugreek relieves gastric inflammation, rickets and anaemia, and recent studies show that the seeds contain a steroidal substance, diosgenin, important as a starting material in oral contraceptives, so this spice could play a part in solving world population problems.

GINGER

Ginger probably originated in the tropics of South-East Asia, an herbaceous perennial plant of about a dozen species, with an aromatic rhizome or underground stem. The plant grows to about 3 feet (90 cm) high, and has leaves measuring up to 12 inches (30 cm) long. Its flowers are clustered in small dense spikes and vary in colour from yellow to green and purple. Harvesting ginger consists of lifting the rhizomes out of the soil and cleaning them; thereafter they are used whole, fresh or dried, or else dried and powdered.

The word ginger comes from the ancient Sanskrit *singabera*, which means 'shaped like a horn'. Ginger was in use in India and China from the earliest times, and became well-known to the ancient Greeks. It was the Romans' second favourite spice, pepper claiming first place in their affection, and ginger appears in several of Apicius's sauces and stuffings as well as in aromatic salts taken to settle the stomach and move the bowels. During the 5th century AD ginger plants were grown in pots and carried aboard Oriental vessels on long sea voyages to spice the sailors' food and prevent scurvy. Ginger reached France and Germany during the 9th century, and England a little later, where it was widely used during the Middle Ages.

King Henry VIII valued ginger highly, and it features in a recipe that he sent to the Lord Mayor of London for a remedy against the plague. Its use in folk medicine, however, dates from ancient Greece, when Dioscorides mentioned ginger's warming effect on the stomach. It has been used in country medicine for stomach disorders, specifically flatulence and colic. It increases sweating and has been used to treat paralyzed limbs, cramps, and as an antidote to poisons. The Chinese used it as a heart-strengthener, and ginger tea was prescribed for delayed menstruation and childbirth pangs.

Ginger is one of the great culinary spices of the world, much used in classic Oriental dishes. For centuries fresh ginger root has been peeled and boiled in syrup to make a Canton speciality, preserved stem ginger. Gingerbread is an example of a traditional recipe that remains very popular. The Tudors added ginger to their punches, served ginger sauce with lamb, kid or piglet, and seasoned fruit desserts with ginger. They spiced black puddings with ginger and cloves, and used it to flavour a delicious-sounding nut jam.

Ginger is widely used today, fresh, dried or ground, to spice sauces, pickles and sweets, to add heat to curries and to flavour ginger beer and ale. In powdered form it is an appetizing addition to a slice of melon, to cakes and biscuits, and to the batter for dessert crêpes. Fresh root ginger freezes very well, and can be grated from frozen for use in cooking.

GINGER FOR TRAVEL SICKNESS

There is an old wives' tale that candied ginger is a good remedy for travel sickness, and even helps to prevent it. So if you are prone to this malady, and if you are partial to ginger, try arming yourself with a packet of crystallized ginger before setting off on your journey!

A MEDIEVAL RECIPE

'Pokerounce' was a 14th-century recipe for thick slices of fresh white bread, which were toasted and spread with a hot honey paste spiced with ginger, cinnamon and galingale. (Galingale is a relative of ginger, with a similar smell and hot, aromatic flavour. It was sold much like its cousin, in dried rhizome form, throughout the Middle Ages.)

PRAWNS WITH GINGER AND GARLIC

This is a wonderful supper dish which is very special but takes no time at all to make. The Chinese-inspired combination of ginger and garlic with soy and spring onion is excellent with prawns and mushrooms. Just serve them on a bed of egg noodles and you have a perfect meal.

1 large clove garlic, peeled and finely chopped
1 inch (2.5 cm) fresh root ginger, grated
4–6 spring onions, finely sliced
3 tablespoons sesame oil
6 oz (175 g) button mushrooms, sliced
12 oz (350 g) shelled prawns
2 tablespoons soy sauce

Sauté the garlic, ginger and spring onions in the oil over a gentle heat for 3–4 minutes, then add the mushrooms and cook until they are well coated with the mixture and heated through – about 4 minutes. Then add the prawns and continue cooking for a further 4–5 minutes, stirring all the time until they too are hot. Finally add the soy sauce, mix thoroughly, and serve immediately on a bed of freshly cooked egg noodles.

Serves 4

JUNIPER

Juniper is a propitious and protective plant, used to avert both evil spirits and the plague. It has been used in folk medicine to treat stomach and kidney disorders, and principally to cure dropsy. They say that an infusion of juniper will restore youthful vigour to the aging! Juniper berries have a very fragrant, spicy aroma and are used to season sauces and stuffings, and go particularly well with rich meats like venison. They are used in pickling meats, in marinades, and in pâtés, and to flavour liqueurs and bitters. Juniper berries give a unique flavour to meat stews, and are delicious in a dish of slowly sautéed, grated potatoes, which is cooked like a hash until browned on the bottom, and served in wedges with fried or poached eggs. Juniper also has an affinity with cabbage, and is often used to flavour sauerkraut. Juniper has given its name to gin by way of its local name *genever*, since the berries are used as flavouring.

These fleshy, three-seeded berries take two or three years to ripen, are almost black in colour when ripe, with a blueish bloom on them. They are collected commercially in Hungary, and from the wild in Yugoslavia and Italy. Juniper branches were used as a strewing herb in the old days, and in Switzerland were burned with fuel in the schoolrooms to fumigate them when it was too cold to open the windows.

MUSTARD

There are three major varieties of mustard which are used as a spice – brown mustard, white mustard and yellow mustard. Black mustard, which is more pungent than the others, is not so widely cultivated; it is less easy to harvest as the plants are tall and drop their seeds very easily.

The mustard plant is native to the Mediterranean, and has been extensively cultivated in China and India from the very earliest days. It is sometimes grown as a cover crop or for stock feed. It is a good cash crop, and the prairies of Canada are now the world's largest producer of the spice.

Mustard is mentioned frequently in the Bible, and in Greek and Roman literature. The ancient Greeks held it in such esteem that they attributed its discovery to Aesculapius, God of healing. The Romans too were great mustard eaters: they pounded it, they steeped it in wine, and they also ate its leaves as a green vegetable. In all probability it was they who introduced it into Britain.

In the early Middle Ages the Arabs introduced mustard into Spain and from there it spread through Europe, and by AD 800 it was being grown on convent lands near Paris to provide revenue for the nuns. In 1336, at a banquet to which the Duke of Burgundy invited Philip the Fair of France, over sixty gallons of mustard were consumed! It became the most popular and widely used spice at this time, and a daily, traditional first course for a winter lunch was a plate of brawn with mustard.

Mustard was sold in the form of little balls until a certain Mrs Clements of Durham, in about 1720, invented a method of preparing mustard flour which was for a long time known as Durham mustard. In 1742 a gentleman named Keen built a mustard factory in London, on Garlick Hill, where he manufactured Durham mustard for about 150 years; the firm was then bought by Colman's who became one of the first, and most famous, firms to sell a product with mass-marketing techniques. One of its offshoots was the bizarre 'Mustard Club' with its 'Order of the Bath' (mustard of course), a light-hearted club which boasted the membership of Dorothy L. Sayers and was terminated by the depression of the Thirties.

Dijon is the most famous name in the history of mustard, and still makes half the world's supply. Since 1937 Dijon mustard has become an *appelation* controlled by French law, just like wine.

Mustard is used extensively in pickles, and makes excellent sauces. All over the world it is used as a condiment for cold meats and sausages, as well as in salad dressings. English mustard is the strongest, popular with roast beef, whereas French mustards are gentler and more aromatic – some smooth like Dijon mustard, others grainy, like *Moutarde de Meaux*. German mustard is a darker version of French mustard, and American mustard is very mild.

A MUSTARD BATH

Mustard is a stimulant and works on the kidneys and on the stomach. It is included in the British Pharmacopoeia in a compound liniment to apply to chilblains and rheumatism. Mustard baths are still sold today after centuries of use, and are said to tone up the skin as well as to relieve aches and pains. They were believed to fend off colds and headaches, and are an effective decongestant and rubefacient since they draw blood to the surface of the skin.

The traditional mustard bath is a foot-bath, and is made by pouring boiling water on to bruised black mustard seeds, in the ratio of 1 pint (600 ml) water to 1 oz (25 g) seeds.

CHICKEN DIJONNAISE

A sauce made with the grainy *Moutarde de Meaux* and Gruyère cheese makes a delicious coating for roast chicken. With rice, and a selection of lightly steamed vegetables, it is a meal in a million.

1 × 3½ lb (1.5 kg) chicken, roasted
2 oz (50 g) margarine
2 heaped tablespoons flour
½ pint (300 ml) milk, warmed
¼ pint (150 ml) single cream
salt and pepper
2 tablespoons Moutarde de Meaux
3 oz (75 g) Gruyère cheese, grated

Cut the cooked chicken into joints and place in an ovenproof dish. Melt the margarine and stir in the flour, stirring over a low heat for a minute or so. Then gradually add the milk, stirring all the time until the sauce begins to thicken. Let it simmer gently for 5 minutes before adding the cream. Season to taste, then stir in the mustard and the cheese. Stir until the cheese has melted, then spoon the sauce over the chicken joints. Heat through at 350°F/180°C/Gas 4 for 12–15 minutes. Serve hot.

Serves 6

Nutmeg And Mace

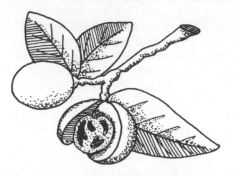

Whole nutmeg is the seed of a tropical evergreen tree native to the Moluccas, the Spice Islands of Indonesia. The fruit looks like an apricot, and at maturity splits in two to expose the red aril cage – the mace – which surrounds a single, brown seed, the nutmeg. The lacy covering of mace is flattened and dried for a couple of weeks in the sun, turning to a tan colour. The nutmegs are dried separately and turned twice daily for 6–8 weeks.

In the 6th century AD nutmeg was recorded as being imported into Constantinople by Arabian traders, and by the 12th century it had reached Western Europe. In England in the 14th century a pound of nutmegs cost the same as three sheep, and in Germany seven oxen. Mace was even more in demand and expensive – by the late Middle Ages one pound would buy a cow!

When the Portuguese discovered the Spice

Islands in 1512, trade in nutmeg and mace became their monopoly for about 100 years. On expelling the Portuguese, the Dutch carried on the trade monopoly – to extremes. In 1651 they planned to uproot all nutmeg and clove trees on islands other than Amboyna, so as to keep the price high. This monopoly lasted until the Moluccas were occupied by the British (from 1796–1802) who introduced nutmeg and cloves to Penang.

In folk medicine nutmeg has been prescribed as a cure for headaches, fevers, bad breath and intestinal disorders. In Arabian medicine it was used as an aphrodisiac, as well as for kidney and stomach ailments. Nutmeg tea was a cure for insomnia but excesses were found to be dangerous, as myristicin, the chemical compound it contains, is narcotic and stupefying and can cause degeneration of liver cells. In prisons, it is known to have been brewed as a 'legal' narcotic for its hallucinogenic properties, and in the Sixties 'nutmeg parties' were the height of fashion.

Nutmeg is mostly used to flavour baked goods, sweets, puddings and egg-nogs, and is added to mulls and punches. It is delicious with fruit desserts, and is also good in some savoury dishes. Mace, with its more refined taste, is used in foods like sausages, sauces, processed meats, pickles and ketchups. It is especially good with fish, and is delicious in a plain cake. Both spices are available whole and ground. Whole mace is difficult to grind at home, but the flavour of nutmeg is infinitely better when freshly ground.

NUTMEG SACHETS

Choose a pretty fabric, either of pure cotton or silk, for your sachet. Make little bags about 3 inches (7.5 cm) across, either by machine or by hand-stitching around three sides.

Fill your bags with the following mixture:

1 nutmeg, grated coarsely
2 teaspoons dried orange peel
2 tablespoons dried rose petals
2 tablespoons dried geranium leaves
1–2 drops bergamot oil
2 teaspoons orris root powder

Then, depending on what shape and size you have made your bag, either slip-stitch along the fourth side and finish with some lace trimming, or tie the neck of the bag with a ribbon.

Use these sachets to scent a clothes cupboard, or put them in a chest of drawers to give your clothes a fresh fragrance over a period of months.

ORANGES IN NUTMEG SYRUP

A hint of nutmeg in the syrup makes this simple dish of oranges a bit different. This is a lovely dessert after a rich meal – refreshing and always popular.

4 oranges
4 oz (100 g) caster sugar
4 fl. oz (100 ml) water
½ nutmeg

Finely grate the peel of one of the oranges. Peel all of them and separate the flesh into segments. Put into a glass dish and sprinkle the grated rind over the top. Make a syrup with the sugar, water and nutmeg: bring to the boil, stirring so that the sugar dissolves, and then boil hard for 5 minutes. Leave to cool before removing the nutmeg and pouring the syrup over the oranges. Serve chilled.

Serves 4

KIPPER PÂTÉ WITH MACE

It always surprises me how delicious kipper pâté can be – there is nothing pedestrian about it at all, especially when it is spiced with mace and freshly ground pepper. It makes an excellent *hors d'oeuvre*, and I often dish it up as an easy lunch with lots of fresh bread and a selection of salads.

2 large kippers
6 oz (175 g) softened butter
a little double cream
2 teaspoons ground mace
freshly ground pepper to taste
1–2 tablespoons lemon juice

Steam the kippers for 5 minutes, covered, until they are cooked. Remove all the flesh from the bones and beat it with the softened butter until well amalgamated. Add the cream and season to taste with the mace, pepper and lemon juice. Pack into a jar or dish and chill. Serve with fresh granary toast.

Serves 6

PEPPER

Pepper is one of the earliest spices known to civilization, and is probably the most widely-used spice in the world today. It is a perennial climbing plant indigenous to the Malabar coast of India where the best quality pepper is still grown. The most intensive cultivation on earth today is in Sarawak, and it is now grown all over the tropics. The vine reaches up to 33 feet (10 metres) in height and has broad shiny green leaves and long 'catkins' of berries.

For black peppercorns, the berries are harvested when they are unripe and still green. They are then dried, which turns them black or dark brown and wrinkled. White peppercorns are the inner seed of the ripe berries, which are red. Green peppercorns are berries which are picked unripe, but instead of being dried are pickled and preserved by canning or bottling.

Pepper became an article of trade in very early days between India and Europe, the Arabs exchanging it for gold. In ancient Greece and Rome, tributes were levied in pepper, and the Romans were particularly fond of the spice: the emperors fattened their incomes considerably by the duty levied on pepper coming in from the East. Pliny complained that by the time pepper reached Rome it was sold at one-hundred times its original cost! At the siege of Rome by Alaric, King of the Goths, the ransom he demanded was 5,000 pounds of gold, 30,000 pounds of silver and 3,000 pounds of pepper. The Romans paid it to him so that he would not sack the city, but he took the ransom and sacked it anyway.

In the Middle Ages payment of rent with pepper became a well-established practice, and a 'pepper-corn rent', which today means a nominal sum, meant quite the reverse in those days. In the 13th century, pepper cost nearly twice as much in England as it did in France – a dear price to pay for the Channel crossing – and a pound of pepper could buy a serf his freedom.

Pepper was instrumental in the rise of Venice as a great empire. It was Venice's virtual monopoly of the spice trade at one time that instigated a search for a sea-route to the Far East, thus influencing the course of world history. By the 18th century pepper was flowing in and out of Amsterdam and London, and in the 19th century it created the first American millionaires.

Pepper stimulates the gastric juices, acts as an aid to digestion and has been added to quinine to settle the stomach. Ancient herbalists used it for fevers, dyspepsia, liver disorders, piles and jaundice, cholera and arthritis. Gerard claims that 'all pepper healeth, provoketh, digesteth and cleanseth the dimness of the sight'.

Pepper is a versatile culinary spice, used before, during and after cooking. It flavours sausages and salamis, marinades and pickles, and is as good with meat as it is with poultry, fish or vegetables. Green peppercorns are used in dishes and sauces to which they add a pungency less sharp and more aromatic than black pepper. White pepper, which is milder than black, is used to spice dishes whose appearance would be spoiled by black pepper, such as a white *sauce à la crème*. Pepper sauces are characteristic of Venetian cuisine, and go wonderfully well with fish, particularly steamed cod cutlets and smoked mackerel. *Steak au poivre* is a masterpiece of French gastronomy, where lightly crushed peppercorns are pressed into the surface of a succulent steak and the meat is sautéed in butter until cooked *au choix* and the juices in the pan are augmented with cream, heated through and served spooned over the steak.

> 'A loaf of bread' the Walrus said
> 'Is what we chiefly need:
> Pepper and vinegar besides
> Are very good indeed.'
>
> *Through the Looking Glass*
> Lewis Carroll, 1832–98

KIDNEYS IN GREEN PEPPERCORN SAUCE

Simplicity itself, this dish of kidneys and mushrooms makes a superb dinner party main course, with its creamy sauce delicately flavoured with green peppercorns. It is mouthwatering served with basmati rice, some lightly steamed mangetout – and a glass of good red wine.

1 lb (500 g) lambs' kidneys, sliced
4 oz (100 g) butter
8 oz (250 g) mushrooms, sliced
2 oz (50 g) green peppercorns, slightly crushed
½ pint (300 ml) double cream
salt and pepper

Sauté the kidneys briskly in the butter, stirring, until lightly cooked. Lift out with a slotted spoon and keep warm. Sauté the mushrooms in the pan and when they are soft return the kidneys to the pan and mix together thoroughly. Add the crushed peppercorns and the cream and stir well over a gentle heat. Season to taste with salt and pepper, and simmer gently for about 1 minute before serving.

Serves 4

POPPY

On Crete an ancient 'poppy goddess' has been excavated with poppy heads on her headdress, showing cuts which make it clear that they extracted opium in the same way as we do today. Morphine, codeine, and papaverine are all derived from the milky juice of the opium poppy, which is an official listed drug. Laudanum, the curse or inspiration (or both) of the Romantic poets, is tincture of opium, a substance with hypnotic and sedative effects. The seeds, however, have no narcotic effects, and possess a pleasant nut-like aroma and taste. They are delicious, and mostly used in bread and bakery goods. A Czech speciality is a light pastry filled with poppy seeds and honey. The flowers are native to Greece and Asia Minor, and come in many different colours – the opium poppy is pale lilac with a purple spot on each petal. The seeds are borne in capsules which open in dry weather.

SAFFRON

Saffron comes from the stigmas of the saffron crocus, a native of the Mediterranean, and has long been cultivated both there and in Kashmir. The spice was taken to Cathay by Mongol invaders, and is today cultivated in Spain, Sicily, Italy, Iran and the 'Happy Valley' in Kashmir. It is a perennial bulb with purple flowers and golden stigmas which are used to flavour food, and as a dye. Saffron is a highly labour-intensive spice, for there is no mechanical way of picking out the three fragile stigmas from each separate flower, and it must be done by hand, a job often given to the elderly. About 75,000 flowers are needed to yield 1 lb (500 g) of saffron – so when you look at 1 oz (25 g) of the spice you are looking at the product of 4,500 crocus flowers! Saffron should always be bought in its stigma form, not powdered, because the latter is often adulterated. Although expensive, the tiniest pinch will contribute a unique flavour and colour to any dish.

Saffron's praises are sung in the 'Song of Solomon', and the crocus was woven into garlands at Persian and Egyptian banquets and religious processions. The Greeks strewed saffron in their halls, courts and theatres as a perfume, and saffron was a royal colour in early Greek times. Homer sings of the 'saffron morn', and their gods and goddesses, heroes and nymphs, were clothed in saffron robes.

The Romans used saffron in their baths, and after a feast would rest on costly pillows stuffed with saffron in the belief that these would prevent a hangover! The streets of Rome were sprinkled with saffron when Nero made his entry into the city, and Cleopatra used it as a cosmetic herb.

Shortly after Buddha died, his priests made saffron the official colour for their robes, which is still the hallmark of his devotees. In Kashmir, growing saffron was long the monopoly of the Rajah, and the spice is still important in Northern India, both in rituals and in food.

By the 13th century saffron was worth more than its weight in gold, and is still the most precious spice in the world. Its high price led to its adulteration, a crime punishable during the Middle Ages by being buried alive. There is a story that during the reign of King Edward III an English pilgrim to Kashmir stole a bulb of the saffron crocus at the risk of his life and concealed it in the hollow staff that he carried. He took it home to Walden in Essex where he planted it, and where it subsequently flourished. So prosperous did the trade become that Saffron Walden, thus renamed, became a free borough in

1694. The three stylized crocuses in the glass windows of the magnificent church that towers over the town are enduring symbols of its once prosperous trade in saffron.

Saffron's medicinal uses included a cure for dimness of sight and jaundice; but above all it was a cheering spice. It made people vivacious and optimistic, too much so according to Culpeper who warned that it would cause 'immoderate convulsive laughter, which ended in death'. In 16th-century England a cheerful, jolly person was said to have 'slept in a bagge of saffron'.

Bouillabaisse is one of the world's great dishes. Made in the South of France, it is a breathtaking combination of fish and shellfish which is lightly poached in an aromatic fish stock. The dish is coloured and spiced with saffron, lightly seasoned with Provençal herbs, and finished with a dash of cream. It is served poured over toasted bread, and with a garlic sauce passed around separately to stir into the soup.

Another national dish, *paella*, a dazzling panful of seafood and rice from Spain, is flavoured with saffron and takes its golden colour from this superb spice. A saffron soup is wonderful, and the spice is delicious with poultry – try a dish of poussin or chicken fillets in a cream sauce tinged with saffron.

SAFFRON SHELLFISH WITH PASTA

Saffron is, in my opinion, the finest of all spices – elusively, distinctively delicate, transforming the dish in which it is used in colour as well as taste. Saffron and shellfish go wonderfully together, and this dish is one of the best party pieces that I know.

12 oz (350 g) cooked mussels
8 oz (250 g) shelled prawns
12 oz (350 g) squid or white fish such as cod
6 oz (175 g) scallops
3/4 pint (450 ml) béchamel sauce
1/4 teaspoon saffron strands
1/4 pint (150 ml) single cream
1 large clove garlic, peeled and crushed

Combine the mussels with the prawns in a large ovenproof dish. Steam the squid or white fish until cooked through – about 6–8 minutes – and remove all skin and bones. Steam the scallops for 2–3 minutes until lightly cooked. Add to the fish in the dish.

Heat the béchamel sauce gently. Infuse the saffron in the cream over a very low heat for 5 minutes, then add to the warm béchamel. Finally stir in the crushed garlic, and pour over the fish and shellfish. Mix together carefully.

Heat through in a preheated oven at 350°F/180°C/ Gas 4 for 10 minutes, and serve on a bed of freshly cooked noodles.

Serves 4

SESAME

Before the time of Moses the Egyptians used ground sesame seeds as flour, and the oil was used by the rich not only in food but in ointments and medicines, and for ceremonial lamps in their temples. An erect annual plant, it bears white or pink flowers and seed capsules which burst open when they are dry. These seeds have a faintly nutty aroma and taste like toasted nuts. They are used on breads and cakes, and are a vital ingredient both of the sweetmeat *halva* and the savoury paste *tahini*. Sesame oil makes an excellent salad oil and gives a distinctive flavour to cooked dishes, particularly in Chinese cuisine. It was used in poultices in the old days, for treating haemorrhoids, genito-urinary problems, and to heal surgical wounds. The Assyrians said that the gods drank sesame wine before creating the earth!

TURMERIC

Turmeric is known as 'salt of the Orient' and was used as a perfume, a spice and a colouring plant from the very earliest times. It was often used as a substitute for saffron, as a cheap dye, and although the taste cannot be compared with that of saffron, it is very good in fish dishes, egg curries, and with rice. It has a pepper-like aroma and a bitter, hot flavour which adds spice to curries and colours them yellow-orange. It gives its characteristic colour to piccalilli, and is usually sold in ground form. It comes from a herbaceous perennial plant of the ginger family, which has a tuberous rhizome or underground stem with a bright orange-yellow interior. These are dug, boiled and dried before being ground to a powder. They say that no ghost can put up with the smell of burning turmeric, so it was used by exorcists!

TURMERIC EGGS

The simplest of supper dishes, this is a lovely golden colour and has the zest and heat of turmeric balanced with the blandness of eggs and rice. Served with a fresh, crisp salad it makes a meal in itself.

1/2 pint (300 ml) béchamel sauce
2 teaspoons turmeric
1/4 pint (150 ml) single cream
6 eggs
12 oz (350 g) basmati rice, washed

Heat the béchamel gently and stir in the turmeric. Then stir in the cream and simmer very gently while you prepare the rest of the dish.

Boil the eggs for 5 minutes and plunge them into cold water. Peel them.

Meanwhile, cook the rice and drain it well.

Put the rice into the bottom of a warmed serving dish and bury the eggs in it. Pour the hot sauce over the top, and serve with a crisp green salad.

Serves 4

VANILLA

Vanilla was discovered by South American Indians long before the Spaniards conquered them in the 16th century, and they used it to flavour chocolate. The Spanish took it home with them and ever since that time it has been used to flavour confectionery, cakes, biscuits and ice cream. In its pure form it is one of the world's finest flavourings, but vanilla essence is an artificial product made with eugenol, extracted from oil of cloves. Vanilla pods come from a tropical climbing orchid native to Mexico. The plant bears pale green flowers capable of being pollinated only by a particular bee or a specific humming bird native to Mexico. Vanilla pods are the unripe yellow pods of this exotic orchid: they are sweated in barrels before being sun-dried and graded. Highly aromatic, vanilla is used in perfumery and for scenting tobacco.

OTHER TITLES IN THE SERIES

The Little Green Avocado Book
The Little Garlic Book
The Little Pepper Book
The Little Lemon Book
The Little Apple Book
The Little Strawberry Book
The Little Mustard Book
The Little Honey Book
The Little Nut Book
The Little Mushroom Book
The Little Bean Book
The Little Rice Book
The Little Tea Book
The Little Coffee Book
The Little Chocolate Book
The Little Curry Book
The Little Mediterranean Food Book
The Little Exotic Vegetable Book
The Little Exotic Fruit Book
The Little Yoghurt Book
The Little Tofu Book
The Little Breakfast Book
The Little Egg Book
The Little Potato Book
The Little Herb Book